ALICE WALKER

A LERNER BIOGRAPHY

ALICE WALKER

Freedom Writer

Caroline Lazo

LERNER PUBLICATIONS COMPANY • MINNEAPOLIS

To Tyler, Chloe, and Cory

Lerner Publications Company
A division of Lerner Publishing Group
241 First Avenue North
Minneapolis, MN 55401 U.S.A.

Web site: www.lernerbooks.com

Library of Congress Cataloging-in-Publication Data

Lazo, Caroline Evensen.
    Alice Walker / by Caroline Lazo.
        p.   cm. — (Lerner biographies)
    Includes bibliographical references and index.
    Summary: Discusses the personal life and literary career of the African American woman who won the Pulitzer Prize for her novel, "The Color Purple."
    ISBN 0-8225-4960-3 (lib. bdg. : alk. paper)
    1. Walker, Alice, 1944– Juvenile literature. 2. Women authors, American—20th century—Biography—Juvenile literature. 3. Afro-American women authors—Biography—Juvenile literature.
    [1. Walker, Alice, 1944– . 2. Authors, American. 3. Women Biography. 4. Afro-Americans Biography.] I. Title. II. Series.
    PS3573.A425Z79   2000
    813'.54—dc21   99-34469

Manufactured in the United States of America
1 2 3 4 5 6 – JR – 05 04 03 02 01 00

Contents

Alice Walker (right) *and her daughter Rebecca Leventhal* (left) *greet fans at the heralded premiere of the film* The Color Purple *in the author's hometown of Eatonton, Georgia.*

Introduction

When *The Color Purple* received 11 Academy Award nominations, audiences around the world were not surprised. The 1986 hit film, directed by Steven Spielberg, featured an all-black cast that included popular actor Danny Glover, television host Oprah Winfrey, and newcomer Whoopi Goldberg. Goldberg, a stand-up comedian at the time, won rave reviews for her first dramatic role. But the real star of *The Color Purple* was Alice Walker, the prize-winning author whose book about growing up black in America's Deep South had inspired the movie.

Walker was the first black woman to win the prestigious Pulitzer Prize for fiction. *The Color Purple* also won the American Book Award, and it stayed on *The New York Times* bestseller list for 25 weeks. Two million copies of the book were already in circulation by 1984 when it went into its 26th printing. But it was Spielberg's movie adaptation two years later that brought the author worldwide fame, as box-office and book sales skyrocketed.

The New York premiere was a star-studded event with searchlights circling the theater. But the special premiere at the Pex Theater in Eatonton, Georgia, where Walker grew up, was the event she would always remember. When she had gone to movies there as a child, she had not been allowed on the main floor. She had to sit in the balcony because she was black. Thirty years later, when *The Color Purple* opened, Walker was welcomed like a queen—with a red carpet, flowing banners, and cheering crowds waiting to greet her.

But hers was no Cinderella story, and no Prince Charming ever rescued her. In fact, Walker's mother was her inspiration.

Walker's readings draw crowds of people who are inspired by her words and beliefs.

Her mother's love and her will to survive—despite their dreary life—is reflected in Walker's writing. Her mother's flower garden added peace and joy to Alice's life and was a constant reminder of the possibilities for change that come with growth—as expressed in *The Color Purple.* "It's hard to imagine anyone in the country this novel couldn't reach," Walker's friend Gloria Steinem said. "The color purple, the most rare color in nature, has come to symbolize the miracle of possibilities."

In the silent beauty of her mother's garden and the mysterious woods behind it, Walker observed nature—every leaf and every creature in sight. In doing so, she developed an early love of the land and all that grows on it. The seeds of both her writing and her activism are deeply planted there.

Slave traders packed Africans into ships to be taken to the United States and sold at auction.

ONE

Out of Africa

*I believe in listening—to a person, the sea, the
wind, the trees, but especially to young black
women whose rocky road I am still traveling.*
—Alice Walker

Even as a young girl, Alice Walker was fascinated by
her African ancestry. She listened carefully to her parents' stories about their family history. It saddened her to learn that
her ancestors had come to America on a slave ship, "packed
like sardines in the hull of the ship." On board, the women
were raped in front of their children, and when the ship
landed in America, all the blacks—including the children—
were auctioned to the highest bidders.

Alice could hardly believe how her ancestors had been
treated in a country that promised freedom and justice for all.
She was amazed to learn that her father's great-great-great-
grandmother, Mary Poole, a slave, had been forced to walk
across the state of Virginia to Georgia while carrying two
babies—one strapped to each hip.

But her parents told her funny stories too. She loved
hearing "Uncle Remus" tales and discovered that her mother
had heard the same tales from her part-Cherokee grand-

mother. Alice wondered if Uncle Remus was a Cherokee Indian rather than an African American, as most people thought. Early in her childhood, Alice sensed a bond between Indians and blacks. Both, she learned, had been oppressed by white people in the United States.

Although slavery had officially ended in 1865, many descendants of slaves still worked and lived in slavelike conditions, and racism was widespread throughout the land. The small, rural community of Eatonton, Georgia, where Alice Walker grew up, was segregated. Black people and white

Segregated cafes were the norm during Walker's childhood and young adult years.

Minnie Tallulah (Lou) Grant Walker (left) *and Willie Lee Walker* (right), *the parents of Alice Walker, in the 1930s*

people lived in different areas, went to different schools, attended different churches, shopped at different stores, and ate at different restaurants. Signs posted above doors specified "Whites Only" and "Colored Only."

Alice Malsenior Walker was born on February 9, 1944. She was the last of eight children born to Minnie Tallulah (Lou) and Willie Lee Walker. The Walkers were sharecroppers—people who farmed the land of white landowners and were paid a share of the crop.

The Walkers had a small three-room shack on the farm, where they raised their large family. Alice's father worked 16 hours a day for $300 a year, and he could never take a vacation. The white landowners, who were former slave owners,

Like this sharecropper family, the Walkers rented land from white landowners.

still controlled their black laborers. Sharecroppers risked being thrown off the land at any time. In spite of the back-breaking work and crowded living quarters, Minnie Lou and Willie Lee Walker found joy through storytelling, singing in church, and other family activities.

Minnie Lou Walker showed her children the great plea-sure derived from planting a garden, but her creative spirit did not stop there. She made all of her children's clothes from rags found around the farm. With leftover pieces of material she made colorful quilts to keep the children warm, and her projects often became a family affair. All the children— Curtis, Fred, James, Robert, William, Molly, Ruth, and Alice—helped their mother assemble scraps of cloth to create the beautiful quilts that kept them warm in winter.

Thoughts of sewing and gardening sustained Minnie Lou while working beside her husband in the cotton fields. Some-

Minnie Lou Walker and her children spent time together sewing quilts for the winter, like the family above.

times she also worked as a maid for a local landowner—often until late at night. Sometimes Alice would wake up on hot summer nights and see her mother outside in the garden, planting sunflowers in the moonlight. She grew more than 50 varieties of flowers on the land behind their little house. The flowers did much more than add color to their shabby environment; they transformed it. She "literally covered the holes in our walls with sunflowers," Alice said.

Where did Minnie Lou's creative spirit come from? How could it flourish in such dire poverty? The answers, Alice believed, were rooted in the past: "This ability to hold on, even in simple ways, is work black women have done for a very long time."

Without realizing it, Minnie Lou illustrated by her own example how to create joy for oneself regardless of one's surroundings. Her children knew that they could open the creaking back door of their little shack and step into a wonderland of flowers. Alice later recalled that the garden was proof that nothing was impossible:

> Because of her creativity with her flowers, even my memories of poverty are seen through a screen of blooms—sunflowers, petunias, roses, forsythia, spirea, delphiniums, verbena. . . . a garden so brilliant with colors, so original in its design, so magnificent with life and creativity, that to this day people drive by our house in Georgia . . . and ask to stand or walk among my mother's art.

In addition to her roles as wife, mother, field laborer, and maid, Minnie Lou Walker was known as "mother of the church." As a little girl, Alice tagged along when her mother cleaned the nearby Methodist church. It was a small, wooden building that a slaveowner's daughter had donated to the black community in 1866, after the ratification of the 13th Amendment to the Constitution ended slavery. In that church, the Walkers and all the other black families in Eatonton could sing their hearts out and feel truly free.

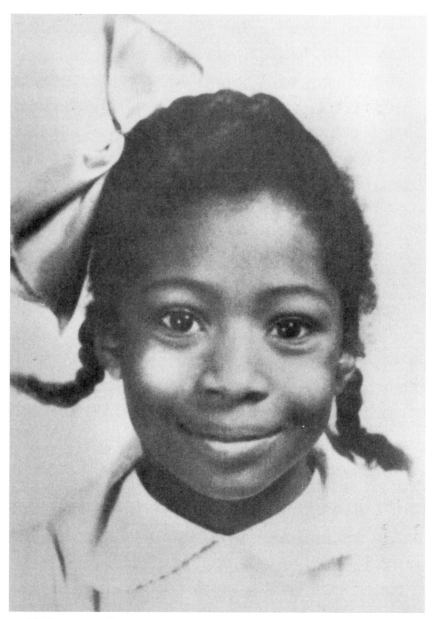

Walker was a happy young girl. People often described her as "the cutest thing."

TWO

Building for the Future

Cleaning the church was a family activity for the Walkers. Every Saturday morning, even four-year-old Alice helped mop the floors, wash the windows, and scrub the outhouse. One Saturday her mother installed carpeting and recovered the chair in the pulpit where the preacher sat. While Alice helped her mother clean the inside of the building, her father and brothers cut the grass and pulled weeds around the gravestones in the cemetery outside. By Sunday "everything sparkled," Alice recalled.

Except for an occasional movie at the little theater in Eatonton, the Sunday services were the only pleasure the Walkers had outside the home. "We spent most of the day in church, listening to the minister, who stood on the carpeting my mother had laid and read from the Bible I had dusted," Alice recalled. Certain stories, such as Daniel in the Lions' Den, The Three Wise Men, David and Goliath, and The Life of Christ, especially captured her imagination. Alice was moved most of all, however, by the singing in the church. She later wrote:

> Because we were Methodists and sang mostly standard hymns, the singing wasn't all that great. I loved it, though, because I like singing with others—still do—and I was, even as a small child, humbled by the sincerity in the voices of everyone. After we sang any kind of song together, there was nobody in the congregation I didn't love.

19

The Walkers spent most of each Sunday at Wards Chapel.

Although Alice was able to understand long, involved stories and was beginning to read, was she ready to start school at the age of four? Her parents thought so, but the landlord—who expected her to work in the fields like her parents—disagreed. Without his approval, Alice could not go to school.

Minnie Lou Walker had had to quit school in fourth grade to work in the cotton fields. She was determined to give her children the education she had never received, because without it their future in the cotton fields was certain too. Alice's father had also left school early to labor in the fields for slave wages, and he wanted a better future for his sons and daughters as well. He had helped win community support to build the one-room schoolhouse in Eatonton. But it was Minnie Lou who argued with the landowner—just as she had done when Alice's brothers and sisters were ready for school.

When it came to her children's needs, Minnie Lou Walker had always won her arguments with the landlord.

"Her quick, violent temper was on view only a few times a year," Alice later recounted, "when she battled with the white landlord who had the misfortune to suggest to her that her children did not need to go to school." As usual, Minnie Lou won the argument. In 1948, Alice entered the first grade.

Though she was the youngest child in the class, Alice excelled in everything—especially reading. She always remembered how her "kindly schoolteacher" made her feel "completely equal to the others." Long before Alice learned to write, she loved to recite the writings of others. "I always tried to give it flourish," she told Gregory Jaynes in an interview for *Life* magazine. And Alice always remembered the organdy dress, white anklets, and patent leather shoes she wore when she performed at school.

In 1950, at the age of six, Alice gave an Easter reading in church. Her perky delivery combined with her big brown eyes and wide smile quickly captured the hearts of the parishioners. "Oh, isn't she the *cutest* thing," she heard someone say.

Although she did not realize it at the time, growing up in a large family had helped to prepare Alice for such moments. She was used to having many brothers and sisters around, and she had to learn early how to make herself heard among them. Living in such close quarters with her parents taught her lessons about adult behavior, too.

Sharecropping was a family effort that involved hard work and low pay, which sometimes made life at the Walker home stressful.

THREE

Family Lessons

Though Alice's father had been a strong supporter of the little black school in Eatonton, he developed a secret fear of education. He was afraid that the more his children learned, the more they would grow away from him. After Alice was born, his health began to deteriorate. Years of back-breaking work in the fields had taken their toll. The once robust, healthy man who felt in charge of his family grew weak—and then impatient, especially with his children.

One day, after a long, hard day of work, he became angry at Alice and her brother Bobby for fighting and making so much noise. Without even asking who had started the fight, he took off his belt and beat them both. Alice's deep disappointment in her father's loss of fairness remained engraved in her mind. At the same time, she knew her father was struggling with obesity, high blood pressure, and diabetes.

As Alice grew older, she came to understand the terrible stress he had been under. As one of the first black men to vote in his town, he had felt both pride and hope for his fellow blacks. He had also helped to organize the poor sharecroppers whose lives were completely controlled by white landowners. But nothing changed. Blacks continued to be dominated by whites, and the future looked as bleak as ever. Even as a young girl, Alice sensed her father's inner rage. That he took time to teach her lessons about truth telling and other valuable building blocks for life made her grateful.

Once, when Alice accidentally broke a fruit jar, she learned an unforgettable lesson in honesty. "Apparently, breaking it was . . . the wrong thing to have done," she recalled. "I could say, 'Yes, I broke the jar,' and risk a whipping . . . or, 'No, I did not break it,' and perhaps bluff my way through." She felt he wanted to hear the truth more than anything else. The minutes that passed while he waited for her answer seemed endless. Finally she confessed. "'I broke the jar,' I said. I think he hugged me." To this day Alice can feel "the happy relief" that he didn't punish her, and in fact, "seemed pleased" with her. "I think it was at that moment that I resolved to take my chances with the truth."

Alice learned lessons from her older brothers and sisters, too. She was very close to her brother Fred, and even when she was a toddler, thought he was her father. He was kind, affectionate, and jolly. It was pure joy to be around him. Alice's older sister Ruth suffered because she resembled Willie's mother, who had been murdered when he was only 11 years old. A man who had claimed to have loved her killed her. Every time Willie looked at Ruth's face, he saw the memory of his mother. That he would reject Ruth for something she could not change was, to Alice, unkind beyond words. Alice would always stick up for Ruth and take her side in any confrontation with their father.

When Alice turned eight, the family moved to a different county and school district. Her brothers and sisters became her best friends, because she felt detached and lonely in her new school. She looked forward to playing with her brothers after school and on weekends. They had fun reenacting scenes from the Westerns they had seen at the local theater— movies starring Hopalong Cassidy, Tom Mix, and Lash La Rue. Alice even liked being called a tomboy, and with bow and arrow in hand, would play the Indian. She would dart from tree to tree and hide behind their makeshift garage, always hoping to outfox her brothers, the cowboys. But one weekend, in the summer of 1952, their play-acting became a scene out of a horror film.

While trying to escape from the cowboys, Alice felt a sudden, sharp blow to her right eye. One of her brothers had accidentally shot her with a BB gun. Both brothers, 10 and 12 years old, rushed to help her to the porch, where Minnie Lou held her in her arms. Alice's fever rose quickly. To reduce the fever, her father resorted to an ancient remedy and wrapped lily leaves around her head. In her book *In Search of Our Mother's Gardens,* Walker would recall that scary, life-altering event:

> They place me on a bench on the porch, and I close my left eye while they examine the right. There is a tree growing from underneath the porch that climbs past the railing to the roof. It is the last thing my right eye sees. I watch as its trunk, its branches, and then its leaves are blotted out by the rising blood.

Alice's older brother, Jimmy, remembered the aftermath of the event: "Well, all I remember," he told her later, "is standing by the side of the highway with Daddy, trying to flag down a car. A white man stopped, but when Daddy said he needed someone to take his little girl to the doctor, he drove off."

Not until a week after the accident did Alice get to a doctor. She left the office with a "glob of whitish scar tissue," a hideous cataract on her eye, she recalled. After the accident, Alice felt more like an outsider in her new school than ever before. It depressed her to learn that the school had once been the state prison—and that the place where the electric chair once sat could still be clearly seen. But students' questions about Alice's eye depressed her more. "What's the matter with your eye?" they would ask. Sometimes the students would do more than ask questions; they would shove her around. No longer was she "the cutest thing." She felt she was just the opposite.

How she missed the warmth and encouragement she had received at her former school! How she wished she could go back there! Tales of misery in the new school finally drove her parents to make a promise: They would send Alice back to her old community where she could live with her grandparents and go to the school she loved. And they kept their promise.

Yet even in her old, familiar school, Alice felt uncomfort-

Western films with stars Jack "Lash" LaRue (above) *and Hopalong Cassidy* (in black hat, facing page) *fueled the Walker children's "cowboys and Indians" games.*

able because of the "glob," as she called it, on her eye. When relatives came to visit, Alice would hide in her room. "You still can't see out of that eye?" her cousin Brenda asked four years after the accident. Alice answered "No," as she had hundreds of times before. No wonder she preferred to stay in her room with her books as her friends. She would stand in front of the mirror and pray that the glob would go away. But she did not pray for sight, she recalled. Alice prayed for beauty. At the same time, she dreamed about "falling on swords" and slashing her wrists.

Feeling more isolated day by day, Alice began to retreat to the peace and quiet of the woods. She loved to listen to the wind rustling through the trees and to spy on the birds and other animals. Alice felt safe and free to be herself in the

Mary Poole, Walker's great-great-great-great grandmother, traveled courageously from Virginia to Georgia on foot.

woods. There she did not have to lower her head for fear of someone looking at her and focusing on her eye. " I felt I was unpleasant to look at," she wrote later. "I retreated into solitude." In that solitude she began to write poems.

On weekends Alice visited her parents and loved their quiet times together. She listened to stories about their ancestors, and it was still the story about Mary Poole's walk from Virginia to Georgia that moved her the most. In Mary's honor, Alice vowed always to keep the name Walker.

During storytelling with her parents, Alice felt completely at home—never the outsider. In church, too, Alice felt at ease. Her parents' friends always made a fuss over her, and for an hour or two, at least, she could forget about her eye.

Segregated businesses were still common in the South in the 1950s.

FOUR

Answered Prayers

In 1958, when Alice turned 14, she received a special invitation. Her brother Bill, who had married and moved to Boston, asked her to visit his family and to baby-sit. When she arrived, Bill sensed at once how Alice felt about herself. He worried that her damaged eye had damaged her self-esteem. So he and his wife arranged for a doctor to remove the white "glob" from her eye. Though a bluish area would remain where the scar tissue had been removed, Alice felt like a new person—filled with joy. She knew she would be blind in her right eye for the rest of her life, but she felt like lifting her head and facing people for the first time in years.

When Alice returned to Eatonton, she began to join friends who were experimenting with cigarettes and cheap wine. They bought them at a local store where the sign above the door read "Colored." Alice bought Kools because her sister did. "By then I thought her toxic darkened lips and gums glamorous," she recalled. "However, my body simply would not tolerate smoke." Because of a chronic sore throat, Alice gave up smoking six months later—"gladly."

Alice looked forward to Saturday night dates with her boyfriend, Taylor Reese. "Now that I've raised my head I win the boyfriend of my dreams," she wrote. "Now that I've raised my head, class work comes from my lips as faultlessly as Easter speeches did." When Alice raised her head, she found more friends than she had ever imagined having.

As she approached her senior year in high school, Alice focused on the future. What would she do after graduation? Her brothers had moved to Boston, and her sister Molly— a brilliant student—had received a scholarship and travel opportunities all over the world. Her sister Ruth had become a hair stylist in Eatonton. Though Alice hated the thought of leaving her friends, her church, and her mother's garden— that had nurtured her in good times and bad—she knew there was a big world out there to see and learn about. Besides, why would she want to stay in a town where blacks were still seen as slaves by the ruling white community? Did she want to stay in a town where blacks were banned from stores, lunch counters, parks, public rest rooms, and even some churches? Did she want to stay in a town where she and her friends were allowed to sit only in the balcony of the movie theater—never on the main floor—because they were black? These questions became more and more important to Alice as her last year in high school drew near.

One day in 1960, while watching the family's small black-and-white television set, a news bulletin interrupted the program she and her mother were watching. A minister named Martin Luther King Jr. was being shoved into a police car in nearby Atlanta. Cameras zoomed in on hundreds of other people who were picketing a store whose lunch counter was reserved for whites only. More people gathered around, and as protesters were pushed into police vans, everyone sang "We Shall Overcome."

That day—October 19, 1960—was a turning point in Alice's life. When Dr. King spoke, he made justice for blacks seem possible. His powerful voice and commitment to non-violent protest captured her heart and mind. "I saw in him the hero for whom I had waited so long," she said. For the

Police arrested Martin Luther King Jr. (far right) *on October 19, 1960, after he staged sit-in demonstrations at segregated restaurants in Atlanta, Georgia.*

first time, Alice saw herself as part of a large movement—the Civil Rights movement—dedicated to changing the United States for the better.

In 1961, Alice graduated from high school as valedictorian of her class. She was also chosen queen of the senior prom. Finally she realized that the students had seen far beyond her scarred, blind eye. They had seen a hard-working, fun-loving friend and a strong, compassionate leader.

Because of her eye injury and resulting blindness, Alice qualified for a special scholarship to Georgia's famous Spelman College in Atlanta. Spelman was known as the best college for black women in America. To Alice, Atlanta also meant the core of the Civil Rights movement and the home of her hero, Dr. Martin Luther King Jr.

That fall, at age 17, Alice left on a bus for Spelman College. When she boarded the bus, she took a seat near the

Martin Luther King Jr.'s followers and fans asked for his autograph during his travels across the United States.

front. "A white woman . . . complained to the driver and he ordered me to move [to the back where blacks were supposed to sit]," she recalled. "But even as I moved, in confusion, anger and tears, I knew he had not seen the last of me."

Demonstrators against segregation—including Walker—continued their protests throughout the United States in the 1960s. In 1964, the Congress of Racial Equality (CORE) and the Student Nonviolent Coordinating Committee (SNCC) protested a meeting of the White Citizens Council in Los Angeles, California (above).

FIVE

Three Gifts

Though Alice's experience on the bus was traumatic, she was grateful to family friends in Eatonton who had raised the $75 for her bus fare to Atlanta. She was especially grateful to her mother who had saved enough money to give her three special gifts—a sewing machine, a typewriter, and a suitcase. Alice would later recall that all three of them were symbols of independence. She knew that her mother earned only $20 a week and must have saved for years to pay for the gifts.

Alice studied hard at Spelman and became enchanted by nineteenth-century Russian writers—especially Leo Tolstoy. She loved the way Tolstoy's characters were rooted in their homeland and how each of them became a distinct individual against a common background. But reading Russian literature and studying for other courses had to be balanced with her growing interest in the Civil Rights movement. At the time, the Student Nonviolent Coordinating Committee (SNCC) was organizing demonstrations in Atlanta to protest racial segregation. Alice looked forward to Saturday mornings when she could join the protesters.

She enjoyed the camaraderie among those involved in the peaceful demonstrations. They came from all over the South to participate in the historic cause. But camaraderie at college was not as easy to find.

Spelman was very restrictive. Alice thought too much emphasis was placed on decorum and curfews. Most students

were content to stay on campus, enjoying the comfortable surroundings. But Alice wanted to do more. Studying hard, she
believed, would further that goal, and it did.

On completion of her freshman year, some Atlanta church
women sponsored Alice as a delegate to the World Youth
Peace Festival in Helsinki, Finland. Before leaving for the 1962
conference, she accepted a very special invitation—to meet
with Coretta Scott King, wife of her idol, Dr. Martin Luther
King Jr.—at the King's home only a few blocks away from
Spelman. Alice and the other students going to Helsinki had
been told by their advisor that Mrs. King "seemed, at that time,
the only black woman in Atlanta actively and publicly engaged
in the pursuit of peace." Alice would never forget the meeting:

> I recall vividly our few minutes in the King home, a
> modest almost bare-looking house. . . . I was de-
> lighted that the furniture was so plain, because it was
> the same kind of stuff most black people had. . . . I sat
> on the sofa and stared at her, much too shy myself to
> speak. I was satisfied to witness her exuberance, her
> brightness, her sparkle and smiles as she talked
> about the peace movement. . . . She did not mention
> her husband, but . . . I couldn't help wishing I could
> sneak out of the living room and through the rest of
> the house, because I was positive he was there.

As Alice embarked on the trip to Helsinki, the Kings were
on her mind. "I have often thought," she said, "that if it had
not been for . . . Dr. King, I would have come of age believing
in nothing and no one. As it was, my life, like that of millions
of black young Southerners, seemed to find its beginning and
its purpose at the precise moment I first heard him speak."

At the Youth Festival, Alice was inspired by the many
programs and seminars that taught her about the plight of
people in Africa, Asia, Latin America, and the Middle East.

Students from all over the world shared their views and hopes for international peace and justice. Following the two-week conference, Alice and other delegates visited the Soviet Union—including Moscow and Leningrad—and stayed in Europe for the rest of the summer.

When Alice returned to Spelman, she found more students participating in local demonstrations to protest segregation in Atlanta. She was proud to join them and to be in the

Martin Luther King Jr., his wife Coretta Scott King, and their children, (left to right) *Dexter Scott, Yolanda Denise, Bernice Albertine, and Martin Luther King III*

presence of rising young SNCC leaders John Lewis and Julian Bond. But Alice soon became worn out from full-time studying and protesting and decided to spend the summer of 1963 in Boston with her brother Bill.

At the end of the summer in New England, she was ready to return to college. En route to Atlanta, Alice made an important stop in Washington, D.C. There, she joined the largest gathering of its kind in pursuit of equality for blacks in America. And there she would see Martin Luther King stand in front of the Lincoln Memorial and give his electrifying "I Have a Dream" speech. From her outpost high in a tree overlooking the memorial, she could see little but heard everything. "I felt . . . not the words themselves, necessarily, but the rhythmic spirals of passionate emotion, followed by even more passionate pauses—roll off the tongue of a really first-rate preacher. I felt my soul rising from the sheer force of Martin King's eloquent goodness."

As her involvement in the Civil Rights movement became more intense, Alice worried that her college work would suffer. After much careful thought, she decided to accept a scholarship to Sarah Lawrence College in Bronxville, New York, where it would be easier to focus on her studies. She hated to miss the Saturday morning demonstrations in Atlanta, but she hoped to find more freedom at the prestigious New York college. Alice's hope became a reality. She transferred to Sarah Lawrence in 1963 and welcomed the open atmosphere of the campus, where she was free to come and go as she pleased. She also welcomed the challenge of attending an almost all-white college. Most of all, she enjoyed the literature courses she took from Jane Cooper and Muriel Rukeyser. She studied the poetry of Li Bai (a Chinese poet), Emily Dickinson, and e.e. cummings. Alice also liked the poetry of Robert Graves

John Lewis, national chair of the Student Nonviolent Coordinating Committee (SNCC), was arrested in 1964 during a demonstration in Nashville, Tennessee.

"because he took it as a given that passionate love between man and woman does not last forever. He enjoyed the moment, and didn't bother about the future."

In Basho and Shiki, Japanese haiku poets, Alice found particular joy. "I ate, I slept, studied other things," she told an interviewer, "[but] it could not change me from one moment to the next as poetry could."

At the end of her junior year at Sarah Lawrence, Alice once again had the opportunity to travel—this time to Africa. She spent the summer of 1964 touring tribal communities, meeting new people, and studying ancient customs. Although the trip was enlightening, she was unable to enjoy the memories of it. She returned to school with bundles of vibrant fabric from Africa—but she also returned pregnant. Fear of her parents' reaction began to haunt her.

Walker listened intently to Martin Luther King Jr.'s words at the famous March on Washington in 1963.

Alice remembered that her father had threatened never to speak to her sister Ruth if she became pregnant outside of marriage, and her mother considered abortion a sin. (At the time—the early 1960s—abortion was a crime.) Soon Alice's old dreams of "falling on swords" returned. She felt alone and full of shame, as she had in grade school. She experienced nausea. Alice sensed no maternal instincts and realized she wasn't ready for motherhood. Taking her own life seemed the only way out. She thought her death would hurt her family— but not if they knew she was pregnant. "They would believe I was evil," she said.

Her memories of Africa—the friendships and landscapes—began to fade, and Alice withdrew into her world of books. Reading and rereading the works of the French writer and philosopher Albert Camus brought her some comfort. "In the depths of winter," he wrote, "I finally learned that within me there lay an invincible summer."

But pregnant and frightened, Alice felt trapped in the depths of winter with no hope of seeing the sun. Three close friends—the only ones there who knew her secret—tried to lift her spirits but failed to do so. Thoughts of suicide filled her mind. She found a razor blade and carefully placed it under her pillow.

Writer and professor Muriel Rukeyser helped get Walker's first book of poetry, Once, *published.*

SIX

New Beginnings

Look: the constant marigold
 Springs again from hidden roots.
Baffled gardener, you behold
 New beginnings and new shoots.
 — Robert Graves

Alice slept with the razor blade under her pillow for three days. All the people and places she loved flashed through her mind. Trees, sky, snow, and sunrise were the wonders of the world she would miss the most. "I was not afraid of death," she recalled. Finally, on the third day of her isolation, a friend gave her the telephone number of a doctor's office. Alice summoned the courage to call the doctor—and to have an abortion. In doing so, she saved her life.

The day of surgery remained forever fixed in Alice's mind, as she later recalled:

> When I woke up, my friend was standing over me holding a red rose. She was a blond, gray-eyed girl, who loved horses and tennis, and she said nothing as she handed back my life. That moment is engraved on my mind. . . . She drove me back to the school and tucked me in. My other friend, brown, a wisp of blue and scarlet, with hair like thunder, brought me food.

Suddenly, and without stopping, Alice began to pour her

heart out in poetry. The poems brought back the joy, beauty, and brilliant colors of Africa. She also wrote about suicide, understanding the roles circumstances and fatigue play in such desperate moments.

Alice was not concerned about having an audience for her poems, but she did want someone to read them. She chose her teacher Muriel Rukeyser as the sole recipient of her work. After writing the poems at night, she would slip them under Rukeyser's door the next morning. "I didn't care what she did with the poems," Alice said later. "I only knew I wanted someone to read them as if they were new leaves sprouting from an old tree."

Alice titled the collection of poems *Once*. Muriel Rukeyser, a poet herself, was so impressed by Alice's work that she gave it to her literary agent, who showed it to an editor at the well-known publisher Harcourt Brace.

A few years later, when Alice was 24, Harcourt published *Once,* and it quickly went into a second printing. The book itself did not seem important to Alice. It was the writing of the poems that mattered to her. "The writing of the poems . . . clarified for me how very much I love being alive," she said. Throughout her poems flowers grow. In "South: The Name of Home," for example, she writes:

> When I am here again
> the years of ease between
> fall away
> The smell of one
> magnolia
> sends my heart running
> through the swamps.

"Exercises on Themes from Life" moves from death to rebirth:

> Speaking of death
> And decay
> It hardly matters
> Which
> Since both are on the
> Way, maybe—
> To being daffodils.

And in "African Images" flowers bloom, despite a nearby snake:

> The rain forest
> Red orchids—glorious!
> And near one's eyes
> The spinning cobra.

Alice's first short story, "To Hell with Dying," followed *Once*. It is the story of an old man and some neighborhood children who repeatedly save him from death. "I was the children, and the old man," Alice told John O'Brien, editor of *Interviews with Black Writers*. In fact, she remembered a similar man—Mr. Sweet—from her own childhood. He was an artist, and Alice's parents had told her that artists deserve the utmost respect. Mr. Sweet was also an alcoholic. He played the guitar, and like a powerful magnet, drew everyone to him. "He went deep into his own pain and brought out words and music that made us happy, made us feel empathy for anyone in trouble, made us think."

When Mr. Sweet died, Alice was still at Sarah Lawrence and could not afford to go home for his funeral. She wrote the story about him instead. At the urging of Muriel Rukeyser, Langston Hughes, a famous and beloved black writer, read "To Hell with Dying." He was so moved by the story that two years later he included it in *Best Short Stories by Negro Writers*. (Later, in 1988, the story was published as a children's book.)

*Writer Langston
Hughes published
Walker's first short
story, "To Hell With
Dying."*

As graduation from Sarah Lawrence drew closer, Alice made plans to return to Liberty County, Georgia, to help blacks register to vote—many for the first time in their lives. That was the "real revolution" in America, Alice said. So, after receiving her B.A. from Sarah Lawrence in 1965, Alice headed south. She and other activists went from door to door, encouraging blacks to vote and helping them fill out the necessary forms. White officials worked hard too—to *prevent* blacks from registering and to mislead them about voting procedures. But Alice and countless other civil rights workers helped to bring about the Voting Rights Act of 1965, which enforced the right of blacks to vote in the United States.

Alice continued her work for the poor by taking a job with the welfare department in New York. But before she left Georgia, she visited her parents in Eatonton. She was sad to find her father ill and to hear him criticize her mother for joining the Jehovah's Witnesses, a religious sect. She saw how destructive her father's domination of her mother had become. Worse, she knew he was not unlike most black people who had been oppressed all their lives. Alice realized how far away from Eatonton she had traveled and how distance had created a new perspective.

When she arrived in New York, Alice moved into one of the poorest areas of the city, the Lower East Side. The apartment was infested with insects, but as long as Alice had a typewriter and a sunny window, she could survive almost anything.

Civil rights leader Medgar Evers was killed in Mississippi in 1963. Walker moved there to "rediscover the South" and to write about the Civil Rights movement.

SEVEN

A Call to Arms

There is always a moment in any kind of struggle when one feels in full bloom. Vivid. Alive. One might be blown to bits in such a moment and still be at peace.
—Alice Walker

Alice worked all day at the welfare department and then worked on her writing at night. She wished she had more time to write. At last, in 1966, her wish was granted. She received her first writing grant—money awarded to a promising artist. Alice had planned to use the grant to go to Senegal, West Africa, but after careful thought, she decided to go to Mississippi—the heart of the racist South. There, she volunteered as a civil rights worker. Medgar Evers, a civil rights leader, had been killed there, and three civil rights workers had vanished while peacefully pursuing equal justice for blacks. (Their bodies were found later in the central part of the state.)

Alice thought she could not work in Africa while there was so much to do in her own country. "I could never live happily in Africa," she concluded, "until I could live freely in Mississippi." So Alice left New York to rediscover the South.

In Mississippi, then America's poorest state, Alice walked through black neighborhoods, talking to residents about the importance of registering to vote. She helped the poverty-stricken, often illiterate, people to fill out voter registration cards and told them about their rights. In *Anything We Love Can Be Saved,* Alice remembered Medgar Evers's murder and other acts of violence against blacks, and she recalled those times:

> In the sixties, many of us were plagued by the notion that, given the magnitude of the task before us—the dismantling of American apartheid—our individual acts were puny. There was also the apparent reality that the most committed, most directly confrontational people suffered more. The most "revolutionary" often ended up severely beaten, in prison, or dead. Shot down in front of their children, blown up in cars or in church, run over by racist drunks, raped and thrown in the river.

While working with the other civil rights volunteers in Jackson, Alice met one in particular who captured her heart—a white law student named Mel Leventhal. The chemistry between them was instant, and they shared a respect for each other's commitment to the Civil Rights movement. But the relationship did not win approval from most Mississippians—black or white. Mel was both Jewish and white, and mixed couples were considered almost criminal in America's Deep South.

Yet Alice and Mel fell in love, and when Mel moved back to New York in the fall to finish law school, Alice went with him. Mel's apartment looked out on Washington Square Park, and when Alice decided to move in with him, he adorned it with fresh flowers to please her.

While Mel finished his last year at New York University Law School, Alice worked on her novel and other writing. She wrote an essay, "The Civil Rights Movement: What Good Was It?" In it she expressed faith in the future for blacks, and praised Martin Luther King Jr. and others who worked so

African Americans formed a massive, snaking line to vote at this mayoral election in Birmingham, Alabama, in 1966. The Voting Rights Act of 1965 gave all Americans the right to vote.

hard for equal justice. In 1967, Alice entered the work in the *American Scholar* essay contest and won a $300 prize.

Next, she received a fellowship from the MacDowell Colony, a community of selected writers and artists in Peterborough, New Hampshire. This allowed her to write full-time in a quiet, peaceful setting. There, in a cabin surrounded by snow, Alice began intense work on her novel. "I labored through a month and a half of snowy winter," she wrote, "the silence of my fir tree-encircled cabin broken only by the tapping of my typewriter, and the singing of Clara Ward and

Mahalia Jackson, which mingled with the crackle of the fire."
On weekends, Mel drove up to New Hampshire in his "tiny
red Volkswagen stuffed to the windows with flowers, grape-
fruit, and oranges."

When her six-week fellowship ended, Alice moved back
to New York, where she and Mel were married on March 17,
1967. When Mel finished law school, the young couple returned to Mississippi to live. Mel worked as a civil rights
lawyer, and Alice became an advisor to Friends of the Children
of Mississippi, a Headstart program. She led workshops in
which she taught teachers how to teach black history. The
challenge was daunting, because the teachers, on average, had
only an elementary school education and little sense of history.

The greatest challenge facing Alice and Mel was of a different nature. Theirs was the first legal mixed marriage in
Jackson, Mississippi, but only the black community, where
they lived and where Mel worked, welcomed them. Whites in
the city cruised around town in hopes of finding and tor-
menting them—Mel for marrying a black woman, and Alice
simply for being black. "We bought a dog and a rifle," she
wrote, "but we depended on our neighbors. If they saw a car
full of strange white people cruising our street they called us,
or stood on their porches until the car disappeared."

Alice found a deep well of stories in Mississippi, especially from the black women who had been so subservient to
whites and frequently abused by black men all their lives. She
listened to their stories and recorded them. She also continued to work on her novel, poems, and essays, while Mel
worked on his law cases. Amid their various activities, Alice
became pregnant. Although she worried about juggling her
jobs, she looked forward to having the baby. On April 4, 1968,
however, all thoughts and activities came to a sudden halt.

Coretta Scott King read a statement before her husband's funeral promising to continue to strive for civil rights.

That was the day Martin Luther King was killed in Memphis, Tennessee, where he had gone to support striking sanitation workers. "When he was assassinated . . . it was as if the last light in my world had gone out," she recalled. "We had a tough, young, fearless friend and brother who stood with us and for us." Suddenly, he was gone.

Mel and Alice attended King's funeral in Atlanta, Georgia, and walked with two hundred thousand other people behind the mule-drawn cart that carried his body. In all the tears and turmoil of the days that followed, Alice lost her baby. It seemed to her that it was a time so filled with despair that "no one deserved to live, not even my own child."

After her husband's death, Coretta Scott King restored vitality to the Civil Rights movement through her own show of

Martin Luther King Jr.'s assassination in 1968 was a blow to the Civil Rights movement—and to Walker. Here, King's wooden casket is carried through crowds of mourners in Atlanta, Georgia.

strength. "Though my heart is heavy with grief from having suffered an irreparable loss, my faith in the redemptive will of God is stronger today than ever before," Coretta King said on television a week later. "She pulled me to my feet, as her husband had done in a different way," Alice recalled, "and forced me to acknowledge the debt I owed, not only to her husband's memory but also to the living continuation of his work."

The cloud of despair lifted from Alice's life, and she went back to work—more committed than ever before. When she discovered later that she was pregnant again, she was filled with hope—hope that this time the baby would be fullterm.

*Walker with her husband Mel Leventhal and their daughter
Rebecca Leventhal in 1970*

EIGHT

Curiosity Unleashed

*Curiosity is my natural state and has led me
headlong into every worthwhile experience
(never mind the others) I have ever had.*
— Alice Walker

Looking back, Alice believed that curiosity had been a driving force behind her decision to have a child. She saw the arrival of a baby as both a mystery and a miracle. Alice thought of a baby as a flower coming to brighten the world. She also hoped that having a baby would keep Mel from being drafted to fight the war that was taking place in Vietnam. The army granted exemptions to many draftees who had children. Alice believed Mel was already fighting a battle—the battle for civil rights. "I still think his draft board has a nerve asking him to join the army," she wrote in her journal on January 2, 1969. "He's already in the army."

Alice felt outrage about the war in Vietnam, as did many other people around the world. Her rage over both wars—the war for civil rights and the war in Vietnam—added to her illness during pregnancy and brought on bouts of depression. She fought her depression by teaching at Jackson State University, recording black women's histories from the women themselves, making a quilt, and working on her novel—her second book.

In November 1969, three days after finishing her novel, Alice gave birth to a daughter, Rebecca. "What is true about giving birth is . . . that it is miraculous. It might even be the one genuine miracle in life," she wrote. Rebecca's "sunniness" delighted her. "It amused me many a gray day when she was an infant and we lived in a dangerous and dreary Mississippi. . . . When I poked my head into the vibrant room, she greeted me with a toothless grin." Alice's anxiety about having time to write while caring for a baby seemed to vanish after Rebecca was born. She wrote whenever possible—day or night. Writing saved her from becoming overwhelmed with anger about the injustices blacks continued to suffer in Jackson and the loss of young lives in Vietnam. Writing became more than a choice; it became a necessity for her.

In 1970, Harcourt Brace published Walker's new novel, *The Third Life of Grange Copeland.* As in most of her work, Walker modeled her characters after people she had known in her past—particularly, in Eatonton, Georgia. She was determined to have her characters speak exactly as she remembered the voices from her youth. Walker wanted them to speak truthfully, as author Zora Neale Hurston's characters spoke. Walker admired Hurston's work from the 1930s "because it spoke the language I'd heard the elders speaking all my life . . . and she [Hurston] did not condescend to them, and she did not apologize for them, and she *was* them, delightedly." Hurston's language was known as black folk talk.

In *The Third Life of Grange Copeland* Walker examines the parent-child relationship—especially the father-daughter connection—and the relationship between men and women:

> I wanted to learn myself, how it happens that the hatred a child can have for a parent becomes inflexible.

Mel, Rebecca, and Alice in 1970

> And I wanted to explore the relationship between men
> and women, and why women are always condemned
> for doing what men do as an expression of their mas-
> culinity. Why are women so easily "tramps" and "trai-
> tors" when men are heroes for engaging in the same
> activity? Why do women stand for this?

Walker's curiosity and boldness were similar to Hurston's,
but reviewers had criticized Hurston because of her free-
spirited lifestyle—not her writing style. Some critics said that
such delight in one's freedom of expression did not become a
black writer. Others claimed that Hurston was not the proper
image for her race. Would Alice provoke the same kind of criticism? Did she dare to reveal herself in her work as Hurston

had done? "And," she asked herself, "if I dared open my mouth to speak, must I always be 'correct'? And by whose standards?"

Alice took the risk and wrote about her past. The novel focused on the effects of economic, political, and social powerlessness on the lives of Grange and Brownfield Copeland. Because her characters did not fit any particular mold, reviewers found it difficult to judge Alice's work by the usual standards. Nevertheless, male reviewers—black and white—lashed out at her degrading portrayal of men and said that Walker had painted young black men in unflattering and often brutal tones, while older men received her sympathy. Walker explained her need to write about blacks in her own way—to show the psychological as well as the social effects of white supremacy on their lives. She tried to show how outside oppression can affect the very core of one's being. A few lines from her poem "Rage" illustrate her feeling:

> In me there is a rage to defy
> the order of the stars
> despite their pretty patterns.

As Walker's writing became a greater part of her life, she needed more uninterrupted time to spend on it. She wanted to develop her next novel and other stories and poems, so she placed one-year-old Rebecca in a nearby daycare center. Daycare allowed Alice to devote several hours a day to writing and teaching at both Jackson State and Tougaloo College.

At Tougaloo, Walker discovered that most books by older black writers were out of print, and she became determined to resurrect them. She was especially interested in the work of Zora Neale Hurston and African authors Bessie Head and Ama Ata Aidoo. Though Walker had never encountered those writers in college, she wanted her students at Tougaloo (and wherever else she might teach) to read their works. Alice agreed with her friend, feminist leader and writer Gloria Steinem, who said, "Perhaps we need to campaign just as energetically to get and keep good books in print as to get and keep good leaders in power."

In 1971 Walker received a fellowship from the Radcliffe Institute, which eased financial constraints for her and Mel. Yet Walker's commitment to writing, working for civil rights, teaching, and raising a child soon became all-consuming, and she had little time to relax. When an offer to teach at prestigious Wellesley College in Wellesley, Massachusetts, came along, she accepted it. At last she and Rebecca could get out of Mississippi for a few months, and Mel agreed that the change would do them good.

Again, Walker's curiosity was aroused. Would she find black writers in the Wellesley curriculum? Would the students welcome her? Such questions flooded her mind as she prepared for her new adventure in 1972.

Walker used Sojourner Truth's abolitionist writings to revolutionize the literature curriculum at Wellesley College.

NINE

Uncovering the Past

Walker was not surprised to find that Wellesley, like most colleges in the early 1970s, had neglected black female writers in its courses. Yet as a leading, progressive institution, Wellesley not only allowed Alice to teach a course on black women writers but welcomed it. Her course became the first of its kind in the country and the forerunner of many to come.

She couldn't wait to introduce her students—mostly wealthy, white young women—to the great female writers who had been overlooked for so long. When she couldn't find their books in print, she duplicated her own copies and stapled the pages together for her students to read. In the same course she taught the writing of Virginia Woolf and Kate Chopin, among others, "because they were women and wrote, as the black women did, on the condition of humankind from the perspective of women," Walker told an interviewer.

Walker's students quickly learned how the brave American abolitionist Sojourner Truth dealt with being a slave and how she felt when she was freed in 1827. The Wellesley students had never heard American history told from a woman's point of view, since most of their textbooks had been written by men. In her own quiet but powerful way, Walker had revolutionized the curriculum, and her students loved the awakening. Walker loved the challenge. "When I am in the presence of other human beings," she said, "I want to revel in their creative and intellectual fullness, their uninhibited social

Zora Neal Hurston is known for her black folk style of writing.

warmth. I want their precious human radiance to wrap me in light. . . . Everything I would like other people to be for me, I want to be for them."

Walker wondered if her white students could accept and understand the writing of Zora Neale Hurston. Would they grasp the truth of Hurston's black folk talk or read it as incorrect English, as so many critics had done? Walker told the students about her own introduction to Hurston's writing and her appreciation of the author's work.

Walker had become interested in Zora Hurston while doing research on the history of voodoo—a term used for a variety of beliefs, traditions, and practices that are derived largely from African religions. Hurston had written about voodoo in *Mules and Men,* and Walker had found the folklore fascinating and absolutely honest. So did Alice's students. They were especially captivated by Hurston's book *Their Eyes Were Watching God* because of its honesty and warmth.

"There is no book more important to me than this one," Walker said.

Hurston had written the book in 1937, decades ahead of its time. The main character in the story, Janie, is a powerful, confident, black woman—hardly a popular topic in white America

Voodoo practitioners boil special broths (left) *and toss a white chicken into the air during a frenzied dance in Haiti* (below).

in the 1930s, or for years to come. In the story, Janie, speaking in the language of the elders, talks about her early life:

> Ah ain't never seen mah papa. And Ah didn't know 'im if Ah did. Mah mama neither. She was gone long before Ah wuz big enough tuh know. Mah grandma raised me. Mah grandma and de white folks she worked wid. She had a house out in de back yard and dat's where Ah wuz born. . . . Ah was wid dem white chiluun so much till Ah didn't know Ah wuzn't white till Ah was round six years old. Wouldn't have found it out then, but a man come along takin' pictures. . . . So when we looked at de picture and everybody got pointed out there wasn't nobody left except a real dark little girl with long hair standing by Eleanor. Dat's where Ah wuz s'posed to be, but Ah couldn't recognize dat dark chile as me. . . . Ah looked at de picture a long time and seen it was mah dress and mah hair so Ah said: "Aw, aw! Ah'm colored!"

Such authentic writing mesmerized the Wellesley students. When Walker lectured on black women writers at the University of Massachusetts in nearby Boston, the book received a similar reaction.

At the end of the school term, Alice and Rebecca returned to Jackson, Mississippi. Alice was pleased to see the progress made by the civil rights workers there. Mel's legal work had helped to desegregate Jackson's schools. Alice saw other improvements too. Restaurant owners had removed "Colored" and "Whites Only" signs from their windows; blacks were not only voting in elections but also getting elected to office; and playgrounds and other public places had been desegregated.

Mel had a personal reason for wanting to win his law cases against the racist policies in Jackson. He told Alice that he wanted to give Rebecca "a completely safe (racially) Mississippi" for her sixth birthday. By 1973 that wish was becoming a reality. Thanks to Mel's work and that of all the civil rights workers, Mississippi had become a safer place for black people.

Writer Zora Neale Hurston (above) drove around the country collecting folktales in the 1930s. As a symbol of admiration, Walker tended to Hurston's overgrown grave.

TEN

The Mark of Zora

When Alice learned that Zora Neale Hurston had died in poverty and had an unmarked gravesite located somewhere in Florida, she decided to find the grave and place a marker on it. Later, in *Anything We Love Can Be Saved,* Walker wrote, "I wanted to mark Zora's grave so that one day all our daughters and sons would be able to locate the remains of a human mountain in Florida's and America's frequently flat terrain."

When Walker discovered Hurston's completely overgrown grave in the Garden of Heavenly Rest cemetery, near Fort Pierce, Florida, she immediately cleared out the weeds that covered the grave, bought a headstone, and had it engraved:

ZORA NEALE HURSTON
"A GENIUS OF THE SOUTH"
NOVELIST FOLKLORIST
ANTHROPOLOGIST
1901–1960

("A genius of the South" is a line from a poem by Jean Toomer, another writer Walker held in high esteem.)

Through talks with Zora's former friends and neighbors, Walker discovered that Hurston had loved flowers and gardening. Alice felt more in tune with Hurston than ever before, and on her return home she wrote an essay, "In Search of Zora Hurston," later published in *Ms.* magazine. With both passion and logic, Walker reminded readers:

> *We are a people. A people do not throw their geniuses away.* And if they are thrown away, it is our duty *as artists and as witnesses for the future* to collect them again for the sake of our children, and, if necessary, bone by bone.

Thanks to Walker's efforts, Zora Hurston's writing was revived on campuses throughout the country. In doing so, Walker enriched American culture.

After her journey to Hurston's gravesite, Walker's writing began to flourish. Like a garden that suddenly bursts into bloom, her books began to appear in book stores. In 1973, *In Love and Trouble: Stories of Black Women,* Alice Walker's first short story collection, and *Revolutionary Petunias and Other Poems* were published.

The New York Times called the stories an "impressive collection," and the book won the annual Richard and Hinda Rosenthal Foundation Award from the American Academy and Institute of Arts and Letters. Two stories—"Everyday Use" and "The Revenge of Hannah Kemhuff"—were included in the *Best American Short Stories of 1973.*

In describing *Revolutionary Petunias,* Walker wrote that the poems were "about (and for) those few embattled souls who remained painfully committed to beauty and to love even while facing the firing squad." The poem that bears the book's title tells about a good, kind woman who kills the man who murdered her beloved husband. Her last words to her children—as she faces the electric chair—speak not of sorrow or regret but of her petunias and the need to water them.

> "Always respect the word of God,"
> she said on her way to she didn't
> know where, except it would be by
> electric chair, and she continued
> "Don't yall forgit to water
> my purple petunias."

Walker based the poem on her memory of a special petunia bush that bloomed wherever her mother planted it. "What underscored the importance of this story for me," she says, "is this: modern petunias do not live forever. They die each winter and the next spring you have to buy new ones." So it is a poem about the enduring spirit, beauty, and love. A stray person—like a stray flower—can bloom wherever planted . . . if cared for and loved. *Revolutionary Petunias and Other Poems* won the Southern Regional Council's Lillian Smith Award for poetry and was nominated for the National Book Award.

But 1973 brought sadness as well as success to Alice Walker. Her father, Willie Lee, who had suffered from bronchitis and emphysema, died of pneumonia that winter. He had stopped smoking toward the end of his life, but it was too late. Thinking about him, Walker wrote, "Daddy, I thought . . . I love you for what you might have been . . . and having learned, too, by now, some of the pitiful confusions in behavior caused by ignorance and pain, I love you no less for what you were."

In 1974, Alice, Mel, and Rebecca returned to New York, where Alice worked as a contributing editor to *Ms.* magazine. Gloria Steinem, founder of *Ms.,* was determined to promote Walker's writing.

That same year, Alice's children's book *Langston Hughes: American Poet* was published. Walker hoped the book would awaken young people to Hughes's poetry and, in turn, keep it alive—just as Gloria Steinem hoped to do for Alice's work.

Feminist Gloria Steinem has been a longtime admirer of Walker's work.

ELEVEN

Discovering Gold

Gloria Steinem had long admired Alice Walker's work and had been especially impressed by her first novel, *The Third Life of Grange Copeland*. The book, Steinem noted, "exposed violence against women years before we had begun to tell the truth in public about beatings by husbands and lovers." As noted earlier, many male critics denounced Walker's boldness, but, as always, she remained true to herself:

> The writer—like the musician or painter—must be free to explore, otherwise she or he will never discover what is needed (by everyone) to be known. This means, very often, finding oneself considered "unacceptable" by masses of people who think that the writer's obligation is . . . to second the masses' motions, whatever they are.

Walker's second novel, *Meridian,* was published in 1976. The book explored life behind the scenes of the Civil Rights movement and described the experiences of those involved with it. The novel exposes injustices suffered by blacks— especially black women. At the same time, it convinces readers that both love and forgiveness between men and women, black people and white people, are possible. *Meridian* received rave reviews.

Walker's success that year was accompanied by sadness, however—the sadness of divorce. Mel and Alice did not disclose the reasons for ending their 10-year marriage, but they remained friends and shared custody of Rebecca. Still, the adjustment to living alone when Rebecca and Willis, the cat, were with Mel was not easy. She was "lonely," she wrote, "with the unexpected grief that only divorce can leave you."

To relieve her anguish, Alice practiced meditation which, she recalled, was "the only thing, other than time, that helped me recenter after my divorce." She also began to think about moving. She thought a complete change of scenery might be refreshing—as it had been when she moved from Jackson, Mississippi, to Wellesley, Massachusetts.

With the help of a Guggenheim Fellowship and a $300-a-month retainer from *Ms.*, Walker was able to leave New York and move to the West Coast. She was sure that California would offer the openness she needed and provide a release from the hemmed-in feeling she felt in New York.

In 1978, Walker moved into a small apartment in San Francisco but found it difficult to write there. A few months later, with the help of Robert Allen, she found the ideal place to live. Allen was an old friend she had first met when she was attending Spelman College and he was a student at nearby Morehouse College. He had since become a writer and editor for *The Black Scholar.*

Walker moved to a small house in the country, in Mendocino County, north of San Francisco. It was the perfect place, she said, "in which to dream, meditate, and write." In that place, Walker rediscovered the world of animals, trees, and "abandoned orchards and undisturbed riverbanks" she had known and loved as a child. "I was in heaven and I knew it. I realized this experience and others like it are the gold and diamonds and rubies of life on radiant earth." With the arrival of her new cat, Frida, the place quickly became home.

> When it is bedtime I pick her up, cuddle her, whisper what a sweet creature she is, how beautiful and wonderful, how lucky I am to have her in my life, and that I will love her always. I take her to her room, with its cat door for her *après*-midnight exitings, and gently place her on her bed. In the morning when I wake up she is already outside, quietly sitting on the railing, eyes closed, meditating.

Walker traveled extensively to attend conferences, sign books, do readings, and protest human rights violations and unfair government policies. On her return, Frida was always waiting for her as she drove up to the gate of the house—"her huge yellow eyes staring out beneath it." She was part of the gold Alice discovered in California.

Walker and her mother Minnie Tallulah in 1979, the year Walker's Goodnight, Willie Lee, I'll See You in the Morning *was published*

TWELVE

The Power of Purple

*Writing about people helps us to
understand them, and understanding
them helps us to accept them as part
of ourselves.*

—Alice Walker

Alice's friendship with Robert—as well as her writing—flourished in northern California. Robert lived in an apartment in San Francisco, but he spent weekends with Alice in the country. Soon they became constant companions.

In 1979 Walker's third book of poetry, *Goodnight Willie Lee, I'll See You in the Morning* was published. The title derived from the last words her mother spoke to Willie Lee at his funeral, just before his burial. Her parents had endured terrible poverty as sharecroppers, and Minnie Lou had had her differences with her husband. At the end, however, she expressed forgiveness in her farewell to him, and Walker captured that spirit in her poem:

> Looking down into my father's
> dead face
> for the last time
> my mother said without
> tears, without smiles
> without regrets

but with *civility*
"Good night, Willie Lee, I'll see you
in the morning."
And it was then I knew that the healing
of all our wounds
is forgiveness
that permits a promise
of our return
at the end.

Writing a poem, Walker says, is a challenge. The process can involve as many as 50 drafts to make it just right. "Like people, some poems are fat and some are thin. Personally, I prefer the short thin ones, which are always like painting the eye in a tiger. . . . you wait until the energy and vision are just right, then you write the poem. If you try to write it before it is ready to be written you find yourself adding stripes instead of eyes. Too many stripes and the tiger herself disappears."

Walker followed *Goodnight, Willie Lee* with her second book of short stories, *You Can't Keep a Good Woman Down,* in 1981. She lashed out at racists and men who took advantage of women, among others, but because she expressed her emotions so freely in the stories, the book provoked mixed reviews. At the time, Walker was more interested in focusing on her next book, her third novel, and she wanted to put all her energy into that project. She had been thinking about the story for years, and at last in the quiet of country living, she began to hear and see her characters come alive.

Just as Alice started to write the book, Rebecca arrived for a two-year stay. Because she was only nine years old, Rebecca would require much of her mother's time and attention. The author hoped she would be able to divide her time between her writing and her beloved daughter. She also hoped that Rebecca would like the peace and quiet of their new home.

Luckily, Rebecca loved her mother's new home in the country, and Alice was able to make time for both her daughter and her writing. In order to focus on the book, she stopped doing lectures and readings. She used advance payments from publishers and her retainer from *Ms.* to support herself. Though Walker had planned to spend five years working on the novel, it took only one year to complete.

Harcourt Brace published the novel, titled *The Color Purple,* in 1982. The story unfolds through letters written by two young sisters who grew up in Georgia, where their parents were sharecroppers. Celie stays in the South, while Nettie moves to Africa and becomes a missionary. By the age of 14, Celie's life has become almost unbearable. She is raped by her stepfather and forced to marry a man so cruel that she never mentions his name—calling him only "Mister."

When her stepfather orders Celie never to speak to anyone about his abuse of her, she writes to God about her life, speaking in black folk talk—the language of Walker's great-great-great-great-grandmother, Mary Poole. Walker modeled Celie after Mary Poole, who had suffered as both a slave and as a woman in the Deep South.

Other characters come into Celie's life and help her to free herself from the dominating forces around her—and even to find beauty in her life. The book's title, *The Color Purple,* comes from a scene in the story in which her husband's former mistress, Shug, befriends her and walks with her through a field of wildflowers. She tells Celie that if one walks by the color purple in a field somewhere without noticing it, God will be angry.

Gloria Steinem sums up the power of the book—and the

symbolism of the color purple—in her essay, "Alice Walker: Do You Know This Woman? She Knows You":

> As always with Alice Walker's work, a pleasure of *The Color Purple* is watching people redeem themselves and grow, or wither and turn inward. . . . What matters is that you don't keep the truth from those who need it, suppress someone's will or talent, take more than you need from nature, or fail to use your own talent and will. . . . The color purple, the most rare color in nature, has come to symbolize the miracle of human possibilities. . . . In fact, it is hard to imagine anyone in the country this novel couldn't reach.

Judging by book sales around the nation, *The Color Purple* reached a huge audience. Major magazines and newspapers praised the book. "Walker dares to reveal truths about men and women, about Blacks and Whites, about God and love. . . . One of the great books of our time," *Essence* magazine reported. *The Cleveland Plain Dealer* called it "A new national treasure . . . a rare and lovely book."

The book's success catapulted Walker onto stages and into classrooms across the country. Her readings and lectures multiplied after she won the American Book Award and became the first black woman to receive the Pulitzer Prize for a novel. Within two years *The Color Purple* went into its 26th printing and translations appeared on every continent.

At the same time, many male critics called the book unfair to black men. These critics believed Walker's black male characters were portrayed as cruel and ignorant. Although such harsh criticism was nothing new to Walker, she was deeply concerned about being misunderstood for so long a time. "I was saddened," she wrote, "that . . . many black men missed an opportunity to study the character of Mister, a char-

acter that I deeply love—not, obviously, for his meanness, oppression of women, and general early boorishness, but because he went deeply enough into himself to find the courage
to change. To grow."

About all of her work, Walker says:

> In my work, I speak to my parents and to my most dis-
> tant ancestors about what I myself have found as an
> Earthling growing naturally out of the Universe. I cre-
> ate characters who sometimes speak in the language
> of immediate ancestors . . . characters who explore
> what it would feel like not to be imprisoned by the ha-
> tred of women, the love of violence and the destruc-
> tiveness of greed.

In addition to her writing and related activities, Walker
became Distinguished Writer in the Department of African-
American Studies at the University of California, Berkeley, in

Walker reading from The Color Purple *in 1985*

the spring of 1982, and that fall she taught creative writing at Brandeis University in Massachusetts. Wherever she taught, she made sure black writers were included in the Women's Studies courses and that women were a part of Black Studies courses. As a "refresher" course for herself, Walker decided to take some time off and travel to China, where women's struggle for equality with men, freedom from poverty, and other issues were similar to those of women elsewhere. In June 1983, Walker left for Beijing, the capital of China.

Accompanied by a group of American writers, including Paule Marshall, Nellie Wong, Blanche Boyd, Tillie Olson, Lisa Alther, and Alice's friend and travel companion Susan Kirschner, Alice made many discoveries in China. She saw the beauty of the people and was struck by the majesty of the trees—"veritable layers of trees five and six rows deep lining the broad boulevards." One is "irresistibly drawn to people who would plant and care for so many millions of trees," she said. She was also drawn to one of China's great women writers, Ding Ling, who headed

Walker was highly impressed with the courage of Ding Ling, Chinese writer and leader of the Women's Federation, shown here in 1980.

the Women's Federation, an organization that helped to counter female infanticide—the killing of baby girls to ensure male domination—by educating Chinese women.

Nearly 80 years old at the time, Ding Ling was still writing, despite the horrors she had endured during the Cultural Revolution in China. The Great Proletarian Cultural Revolution, launched in 1966 by Mao Zedong, was designed to prevent the rise of a ruling class in China. After being imprisoned and "beaten bloody" for expressing her views regarding the oppression of women and the violation of basic human rights in her country, Ding Ling harbored no bitterness. She only lamented the time lost. "Oh, to be 67 again!" she told Alice. Few people impressed Walker as deeply as Ding Ling did. Other examples of such courage and triumph would be hard to find.

In China, Walker realized that the struggle for women to affirm solidarity with other women is universal, and their struggle for equal justice has no boundaries. When a Shanghai magazine editor told Walker that *The Color Purple* was "a very Chinese story," she understood the universality of the book's message. It was no longer just a story about growing up black and female in America's South. It was about oppression of women—and others—everywhere, and about the power to change.

When Walker returned to California, she was anxious to get back to her writing. Questions from readers were pouring in from all over the world. Some even wondered if *The Color Purple* might make a good movie, but that was the furthest thing from her mind. Alice looked forward to being with Rebecca and Robert again and to planting a hundred fruit trees on her land!

In The Color Purple, *Celie (Whoopie Goldberg,* left) *and Shug (Margaret Avery,* right) *read letters accumulated over many years from Celie's sister. Mister had hidden them under the floorboards of his house.*

THIRTEEN

Welcome Home, Alice Walker

In light of her growing popularity, Walker's editor asked her to compile a collection of essays about her life. She was happy to do so, and when she put the essays together, they served as a kind of autobiography. She titled the collection *In Search of Our Mothers' Gardens: Womanist Prose.* Walker used the word *womanist* instead of feminist because she thought it was stronger and had more depth. "Womanist is to feminist as purple is to lavender," she said.

The essays, many of which had been published in magazines, describe memorable moments in Walker's life. People who had had a special impact on her life—family, friends, civil rights leaders, lost-and-found women writers—animate the book.

While trying to spend more time at home and less in the literary spotlight, Walker received the news that director Steven Spielberg wanted to make a movie of *The Color Purple.* With Walker as his chief consultant, the noted film director felt sure that the movie would be both authentic and successful. But Alice worried about a Hollywood version of her heartfelt story. Finally, after consulting with close friends, she agreed to let Spielberg buy the rights to make the movie. She realized that many people who couldn't (or wouldn't) read the book could share her story on the screen. When

Spielberg asked Walker to help select the cast, she was delighted.

Walker chose Whoopi Goldberg to play Celie. Goldberg had been performing as a comedian, had never before made a movie, and was not well known. Margaret Avery played Shug, and the leading male roles went to Danny Glover and Adolph Caesar. Talk show host Oprah Winfrey also starred in the film.

In 1984, just prior to the filming of *The Color Purple,* Walker's third collection of poems, *Horses Make a Landscape More Beautiful,* was published and received high praise. The book branches out from black women's struggles to address other issues that are important to Walker. In her poem "Who?" she alerts her readers to the environment and the

Sophie (Oprah Winfrey) turns from outspoken to silent and depressed after spending years in prison for assaulting a white man.

Mister (Danny Glover, above*) watches over his fields in a rage. Glamorous Shug* (right) *sings "Miss Celie's Blues" to an enamored crowd at Harpo's bar.*

damage the *Wasichus* have done to it. Wasichus is a Sioux word for white people, but in a broader sense the term refers to anyone who is greedy and destructive. Walker's interest in Native Americans stems from her own heritage—namely Tallulah, her great-grandmother on her mother's side, who was part Cherokee. Knowing one's ancestors, Walker believes, helps us to know ourselves. Other topics in *Horses*

Walker (left) *accepted a Purple Globe Award from singer Tom Waits* (right) *after receiving the Pulitzer Prize for Literature in 1986.*

include poverty, materialism, violence, the value of family and friends, and the importance of writing to provide balance in life.

Out of concern for talented but unknown writers, Walker and Allen formed a small publishing company called Wild Trees Press. Their purpose was to publish only a few books a year and to introduce such authors to readers.

In December 1985 the movie version of *The Color Purple* opened to great fanfare in New York. But the January 18th premiere in Walker's hometown of Eatonton, Georgia, was more important to her. Alice's sister Ruth Walker Hood had arranged a special celebration for the premiere. A banner that read "Welcome Home Alice Walker" hung across the town's main street, and lights flashed everywhere. A red carpet lined the entrance to the Pex Theater. Walker could hardly believe what she was seeing.

That year the movie earned 11 Academy Award nominations—including one for Best Picture. Though *Out of Africa* won the Best Picture Award, *The Color Purple*—and Alice Walker—had attracted new audiences all over the world. Book sales multiplied, and once again it topped best-seller lists. Most important, because of the movie, Walker's story had reached people in remote parts of the world, many of whom were unable to read. From the beginning, that had been her goal.

Robert Allen and Walker protested the U.S. government's shipment of weapons to Central America in 1987 at Concord Naval Weapons Station, Concord, California.

FOURTEEN

Passions and Commitments

Love cures people,
the ones who receive
love and the ones
who give it, too.
—Karl A. Menninger

In 1987, Robert gave Alice a trip to Bali, an island in the South Pacific, as a birthday present. She basked in the sun and enjoyed the flowers, dances, and rituals of the people there. But it was the sight of a chicken crossing a road that left the most lasting impression on her.

Walker had been on the brink of becoming a vegetarian, but seeing the chicken inspired her to commit to the diet. When she saw the chicken—with "quick, light brown eyes"— marching its chicks across a road, Walker realized that it was caring for its offspring just as she cared for hers. Walker asked herself, how could anyone kill them—or any living creatures—for one's own eating pleasure?

"I console myself," she wrote, "by recognizing that this diet, in which ninety percent of what I eat is nonmeat and nondairy, though not pristinely vegetarian, is still completely different from . . . the one I was raised on—in which meat was a mainstay." Her essay "Why Did the Balinese Chicken Cross the Road?" was published in *Women of Power* the following year.

On their return to California, Alice and Robert organized a protest against the shipment of American weapons to Central America for use against the people's uprisings there. The protest took place at the Concord Naval Weapons Station in Concord, California, on June 12, 1987.

When asked why she was willing to risk arrest, Alice replied: " . . . because I can't stand knowing that the money I pay in taxes . . . pays for weapons and the policy that maims, kills, frightens, and horribly abuses babies, children, women, men, and the old. I don't want to be a murderer. . . . " Hundreds of others agreed with her and—like Walker—were arrested for their cause.

Walker after her arrest at Concord Naval Weapons Station

Walker read The Temple of My Familiar *for the novel's audiobook.*

Walker addressed many of her social and political concerns in *Living by the Word,* her second book of essays, published in 1988. As far back as she can remember, Walker has worried about the earth and "the wanton dumpings of lethal materials all across its proud face and in its crystal seas." Other subjects in the book address some of Walker's passions and commitments, including feminism, personal relationships, travel, and activism. *The New York Times* described it as "an inspired and thoughtful collection by a woman who has not chosen to rest on her much-deserved laurels."

After *Living by the Word,* Walker completed her fourth novel, *The Temple of My Familiar.* This book, which she had been working on for eight years, was published in 1989. She wrote the "romance of the last 500,000 years," because she wanted to revive some of the characters from *The Color Purple.* The story sweeps across the United States, England, Latin America, and Africa and delves into ancestral lives and relationships. When asked what characters she played in the story, she replied: "I'm everywhere and I'm everybody. That's true in all my books."

There is no doubt that Alice Walker is everywhere in her fifth book of poetry, *Her Blue Body Everything We Know: Earthling Poems 1965–1990 Complete.* The "Blue Body" stands for the planet Earth. "The Earth," Walker reminds us, "is our Mother. . . . She must be honored in order for our days to be long on this planet." *Her Blue Body* and a children's book titled *Finding the Green Stone* were both published in 1991.

Walker's next book, *Possessing the Secret of Joy,* was a novel that dealt with the controversial, socio-political issue of female circumcision, a custom that is practiced in parts of Africa, Southeast Asia, and the Middle East as part of ancient traditions and religious rites. Walker—and most human rights supporters in Western countries—view the custom as a form of female genital mutilation. Walker acknowledged that the subject was unpopular, ancient, and taboo, but she made a commitment to confront it head-on. She wanted the world to know the great physical and psychological damage such practices cause women and girls, and she hoped the book might help put an end to it.

Possessing the Secret of Joy, published in 1992, got mixed reviews. *The New York Times Book Review* proclaimed that "Alice Walker is a lavishly gifted writer," but other reviewers criticized the way Walker blanketed her political beliefs in a work of fiction. The author felt so strongly about the subject, however, that she made a documentary with London-based filmmaker Pratibha Parmar. The film *Warrior Marks,* based on Walker's book *Warrior Marks: Female Genital Mutilation and the Sexual Binding of Women,* debuted in the United States in 1993.

Walker reading from The Same River Twice: Honoring the
Difficult *in 1996*

FIFTEEN

Love in Action

*My activism—cultural, political, spiritual—
is rooted in my love of nature and my delight
in human beings.*

—Alice Walker

In 1994 Walker won the California Governor's Award for Literature, but she spent little time basking in the glow of fame and success. That spring the United States and Cuba Project, a humanitarian organization, asked Walker to lead a delegation of women who would bring a supply of antibiotics valued at five million dollars to the Cuban people. Walker agreed immediately. Cuba was, after all, a neighbor, located only 90 miles from Florida's coast. In 1962, the Kennedy administration had imposed a full trade embargo on Cuba, because it was convinced that President Fidel Castro was moving the country toward a totalitarian regime with help from the Soviet Union—then a foe of the United States. The U.S. government had hoped that the embargo would cause Castro to abandon communism in favor of American-style democracy. But the hardship the embargo caused the Cuban people—especially the children—outraged Alice and many other Americans. Even Pope John Paul II, on his historic visit to Cuba in 1997, harshly criticized the U.S. embargo and called it "ethically unacceptable."

While in Havana, Walker talked to Cuban families and tried to lift their spirits. She and her delegation also met with President Castro, who thanked them for their special act of kindness. "I've often asked myself," Walker wrote, "how a strong, well-fed, militarily secure nation like the United States could demean itself by torturing a small country like Cuba, just because its leader refuses to knuckle under."

Walker's humanitarian efforts continued throughout the 1990s. In 1996 she attended a human rights awareness conference in Bolgatanga, Ghana. She met with African men and women committed to abolishing female genital mutilation, and, as she did in Cuba, Walker listened to people's stories.

At home in northern California, Alice continues to work

Walker (second from left) *and members of the Cuba Project met President Fidel Castro* (third from right) *in 1995.*

Walker continues to give readings and to sign books for admirers. Here, she signs copies of The Same River Twice: Honoring the Difficult.

for her favorite organizations, including The Color Purple Education Foundation and the Ms. Foundation for Women of New York "to assist feminist publishing." Walker herself writes nonstop. *The Same River Twice: Honoring the Difficult,* published in 1996, and *Anything We Love Can Be Saved,* published in 1997, add to the impressive list of Walker's books. In *Anything We Love,* her activism—"rooted in love"—is ever present. Covering subjects from the environment to embargoes, the collection of essays reflects her passion for justice and peace. *By the Light of My Father's Smile* was published in1998.

Walker loves to listen to and guide young black women whenever she can. Her speech to the 1995 graduating class at

Spelman College will long be remembered. Her closing words ring with the eloquence, wisdom, and love that make Alice Walker so appreciated around the world:

> I give you my word that I shall continue to struggle for and with you, to think of and work for your well-being as women of color, constantly. . . . To affirm your strength of character wherever I find myself. . . . To honor your beauty and to believe in you without reservation.
>
> I know from experience that you are good, and that the world is only made better by your presence.
>
> I love you.

Alice still finds paradise in northern California, where, like her mother's petunias (and in part because of them), she continues to bloom.

Sources

pp. 8–9   Gloria Steinem, *Outrageous Acts and Everyday Rebellions* (New York: Holt, Rinehart and Winston, Second Ed. 1995), 292.

p. 11   Alice Walker quoted in Paula Giddings, "Alice Walker's Appeal," *Essence*, July 1992, 60.

p. 16   Alice Walker, *In Search of Our Mothers' Gardens* (San Diego: Harcourt Brace & Company, 1983), 242.

p. 16   Ibid., 238–139.

p. 16   Ibid., 241.

p. 19   Alice Walker, *Anything We Love Can Be Saved* (New York: Random House, 1977), 18.

p. 19   Ibid., 11.

p. 21   Alice Walker, *In Search of Our Mothers' Gardens,* 238.

p. 21   Alice Walker quoted in Gregory Jaynes, "Living by the Word," *Life,* May 1989, 62.

p. 24   Alice Walker, *Living by the Word* (San Diego: Harcourt Brace & Company, 1988), 12.

p. 25   Alice Walker, *In Search of Our Mothers' Gardens,* 364.

p. 25   Ibid., 365.

p. 28   Alice Walker quoted in John O'Brien. "Alice Walker," *Interviews with Black Writers* (New York: Liveright, 1973), 187.

p. 31   Alice Walker, *Living by the Word,* 122.

p. 31   Alice Walker, *In Search of Our Mothers' Gardens,* 367.

p. 32   Ibid., 124.

p. 35   Ibid., 163.

p. 38   Ibid., 146–147.

p. 40   Ibid., 159.

p. 41   Alice Walker quoted in O'Brien, 198.

p. 41   Ibid., 199.

p. 42   Ibid., 188.

p. 43   Albert Camus, *Lyrical and Critical Essays* (New York: Vintage Books, 1970), 169.

p. 45   Alice Walker quoted in O'Brien, 189.

p. 45   Ibid.

p. 46   Ibid., 190.

p. 46   Ibid.

p. 46   Alice Walker, *Once* (San Diego: Harcourt Brace & Company, 1968), 39.

p. 47   Ibid., 79.

p. 47   Ibid., 5.

p. 47   Alice Walker quoted in O'Brien, 190.

p. 51   Alice Walker, *In Search of Our Mothers' Gardens,* 163.

p. 52   Alice Walker, *Anything We Love Can Be Saved,* xxii.

p. 53   Alice Walker, *The Third Life of Grange Copeland* (New York: Washington Square Press, 1988), 341.

p. 54   Ibid., 342.

p. 54   Alice Walker, *In Search of Our Mothers' Gardens,* 192.

p. 55   Ibid., 147.

p. 57   Ibid., 148.

p. 59   Ibid., 377.

p. 60   Ibid.

p. 60   Alice Walker, *Anything We Love Can Be Saved,* 46.

pp. 60–61   Alice Walker quoted in O'Brien, 197.

p. 62   Alice Walker, *In Search of Our Mothers' Gardens,* 87.

p. 62   Alice Walker, *Revolutionary Petunias* (San Diego: Harcourt Brace & Company, 1973), 61.

p. 63   Gloria Steinem, *Outrageous Acts and Everyday Rebellions,* 300.

pp. 65–66   Alice Walker, *Anything We Love Can Be Saved,* xxii.

p. 67   Alice Walker, *In Search of Our Mothers' Gardens,* 86.

p. 68   Zora Neale Hurston, *Their Eyes Were Watching God* (New York: Harper & Row, 1937, 1990), 8-9.

p. 69   Alice Walker, *In Search of Our Mothers' Gardens,* 167.

p. 71   Alice Walker, *Anything We Love Can Be Saved,* 47.

p. 72   Alice Walker, *In Search of Our Mothers' Gardens,* 92.

p. 72   Alice Walker, *Revolutionary Petunias,* Preface.

p. 73   Alice Walker quoted in O'Brien, 208.

p. 73   Alice Walker, *Living by the Word,* 17.

p. 75   Gloria Steinem, *Outrageous Acts and Everyday Rebellions,* 300.

p. 76   Alice Walker, *Anything We Love Can Be Saved,* 129.

p. 76   Ibid., 95.

p. 76   Ibid., 130.

p. 77   Ibid., 133.

pp. 79–80   Ibid., 104.

p. 80   Alice Walker quoted in O'Brien, 210–211.

p. 82   Gloria Steinem, *Outrageous Acts and Everyday Rebellions,* 283.

pp. 82–83   Alice Walker, *Living by the Word,* 80.

p. 83   Alice Walker, *Anything We Love Can Be Saved,* 4.

p. 84   Alice Walker, *Living by the Word,* 109.

p. 85   Ibid.

p. 87   Alice Walker, *In Search of Our Mothers' Gardens,* back cover.

p. 93   Alice Walker, *Living by the Word,* 172.

p. 93   Ibid.

p. 94   Ibid., 182.

p. 95   Ibid., 147.

p. 96   Alice Walker quoted in Jaynes, 63.

p. 96   Alice Walker, *Anything We Love Can Be Saved,* 106.

p. 99   Quoted by News Services, *Star Tribune,* Minneapolis, Jan. 26, 1997 A9.

p. 100   Alice Walker, *Anything We Love Can Be Saved,* 208.

p. 102   Ibid., 107.

Bibliography

Bloom, Harold, ed. *Alice Walker.* New York: Chelsea House, 1989.

Camus, Albert. *Lyrical and Critical Essays.* New York: Vintage Books, 1970.

Cooke, Michael G. *Afro-American Literature in the Twentieth Century.* New Haven: Yale University Press, 1984.

Dudley, Karen, and Pat Rediger. *Outstanding African Americans.* New York: Crabtree Publishing Company, 1996.

Evans, Mari, ed. *Black Women Writers.* Garden City, New York: Doubleday, 1984.

Gates, Henry Louis Jr., and K.A. Appiah, eds. *Alice Walker: Critical Perspectives Past and Present.* New York: Amistad Press, 1993.

Giddings, Paula. "Alice Walker's Appeal." *Essence,* July 1992.

Hurston, Zora Neale. *Their Eyes Were Watching God.* New York: Harper & Row, 1937, 1990.

Igus, Toyomi, ed. *Book of Black Heroes, Vol. 2: Great Women in the Struggle.* New York: Scholastic Inc., 1991.

Jaynes, Gregory. "Living by the Word." *Life,* May 1989.

O'Brien, John. "Alice Walker." *Interviews with Black Writers.* New York: Liveright, 1973.

Steinem, Gloria. "Do You Know This Woman? She Knows You: A Profile of Alice Walker." *Outrageous Acts and Everyday Rebellions.* New York: Holt, Rinehart and Winston (Second Edition), 1995.

Walker, Alice. *Anything We Love Can Be Saved.* New York: Random House, 1997.

——————. *The Color Purple.* San Diego: Harcourt Brace & Company, 1982.

——————. *Living by the Word.* San Diego: Harcourt Brace & Company, 1988.

——————. *Meridian.* New York: Washington Square Press, 1977.

——————. *Once.* San Diego: Harcourt Brace & Company, 1968.

——————. *Possessing the Secret of Joy.* New York: Washington Square Press, 1992.

——————. *Revolutionary Petunias.* San Diego: Harcourt Brace & Company, 1973.

——————. *In Search of Our Mothers' Gardens.* San Diego: Harcourt Brace & Company, 1983.

——————. *The Temple of My Familiar.* New York: Washington Square Press, 1990.

——————. *The Third Life of Grange Copeland.* New York: Washington Square Press, 1988.

Washington, Mary Helen. "Alice Walker: Her Mother's Gifts." *Ms.,* June 1982.

Winchell, Donna Haisty. *Alice Walker.* New York: Twayne Publishers, 1992.

Index

Walker often gives speeches at universities. Here she smiles at Harvard University in 1993.

For Further Reading in Lerner Books

Gloria Steinem: Feminist Extraordinaire
by Caroline Lazo

Martin Luther King Jr.
by Joan Darby

Maya Angelou
by L. Patricia Kite

Slave Young Slave Long: The American Slave Experience
by Meg Greene

Voices of Feminism: Past, Present, and Future
by JoAnn Bren Guernsey

About the Author

Caroline Lazo has written numerous biographies of men and women who have broken down barriers of race, religion, and gender to achieve equality for struggling peoples around the world. Her works include *Gloria Steinem: Feminist Extraordinaire,* and *Arthur Ashe,* a Notable Children's Trade Book selection of the National Council for Social Studies, also published by Lerner Publications Company.

Photo Acknowledgments

Photographs have been reproduced with permission from: Alice Walker, pp. 2, 13, 18, 20, 28, 58, 78, 100; UPI/Corbis-Bettmann, pp. 6, 14, 42, 61; © Steve Jennings/Corbis, p. 8; Archive Photos, pp. 10, 12, 26, 27, 30, 44, 67 (left); Library of Congress (USF34-25363), p. 15; Corbis/Bettmann-UPI, pp. 22, 33, 36, 41, 55, 83; Washington Post; reprinted by permission of the D.C. Public Library, p. 34; Martin Luther King Jr. Center for Nonviolent Social Change, Inc., p. 39; AP/Wide World Photos, pp. 48, 53, 56, 67 (right), 74, 95; © Carl Robinson/Globe Photos, Inc., p. 50; Independent Picture Service, p. 64; Corbis, pp. 66, 90; Unknown, p. 70; © ChinaStock, p. 84; Globe Photos, Inc., pp. 86, 89 (right); Hollywood Book and Poster, p. 88; Warner Bros./Archive Photos, p. 89 (left); Belvie Rooks, p. 92; © Jon McNally, p. 94; © Andrea Renault/Globe Photos, Inc., pp. 98, 101; Ilene Perlman/Impact Visuals, p. 107.

Cover: © Adam Scull/Globe Photos, Inc.